"Bee's narrative is an exploration of humanity by observation. They bring you along their journey, dissecting the lives of those they meet in a compassionate but rigidly honest manner. Their work is reminiscent of Anne Sexton; conventional, touching on the vulnerable topics of sexuality and violations, religion and opposition, and the dangers of being a human in day to day life. Yet, Bee manages this in a light, almost playful presentation, curbing dread in favor of brief moments of anger and the occasional detached shock.

Every space, every font change, every modality, means something in this narrative, and it is up to the reader to fill in what is left unsaid, but still communicated. Themes of oneness and unity conflict with alienation and stark sensation of aloneness." –Ruby

"Right off the bat I was really struck by the way you talked about your room. It took me back to my teenage years and early 20s when I used to spend hours in my room and I would just feel trapped and scared. And I felt sad imagining the pain you felt while you were selling your body. Just imagining you so young and going through so much just broke my heart. But afterwards I felt your excitement for life, the way you learned to love yourself and fight for yourself. I felt your exhilaration as you rode your bike after your yoga class, I could feel the wind in my face. I love the way you seem to be a part of the land. I love how you can just be." –Oscar

The Poemographies of Lee

After High School &
When Jesus Took Me to Roosevelt

Lee Bee

BALBOA.PRESS
A DIVISION OF HAY HOUSE

Balboa Press books may be ordered through booksellers or by contacting:

Balboa Press
A Division of Hay House
1663 Liberty Drive
Bloomington, IN 47403
www.balboapress.com
844-682-1282

Because of the dynamic nature of the Internet, any web addresses or
links contained in this book may have changed since publication and
may no longer be valid. The views expressed in this work are solely those
of the author and do not necessarily reflect the views of the publisher,
and the publisher hereby disclaims any responsibility for them.

The author of this book does not dispense medical advice or prescribe the use
of any technique as a form of treatment for physical, emotional, or medical
problems without the advice of a physician, either directly or indirectly. The
intent of the author is only to offer information of a general nature to help
you in your quest for emotional and spiritual well-being. In the event you use
any of the information in this book for yourself, which is your constitutional
right, the author and the publisher assume no responsibility for your actions.

Print information available on the last page.

ISBN: 979-8-7652-5335-9 (sc)
ISBN: 979-8-7652-5336-6 (e)

Balboa Press rev. date: 08/21/2024

These are autobiographies in poetry.

Boundaries : A Proclamation

Please,

My art isn't to please you.

I am open to questions.

Unless I don't want to answer them.

I walk a fine line between tmi.

Con Amore,

leeb

After High School discuses

drugs,
suicide,
and   sex

and
is written in   Shadowwriting format
which means that

I took the darkest most
painful parts of

My Fucking Journey

and wrote them in this
Poemography.

So skip ahead to the next one if you'd like.

Take This Journey With Me . . .

Is taking yourself back to heal a fine line?
Or is now the only time?

Maybe just for the show,
I'll take myself back to clearly know

The exact places where I've grown,
and see what skin I didn't show.

How I Learnt of My Importance, and Yours

During high school, a string of oppression

and lack of expression led to great

loneliness and internal despair.   Looking like external repair . . .

Reaching out   and out,

further and further from myself and my life,   of life.

What is it and why won't anyone help?

                                        Suicide attempt.

                    Then,

                                        Heartbreak.

The Room

I was stored in a very large room.
I am wondering now of the doom
creating a bigger picture, zooomed;
that I, only I, now knew.

I couldn't have had a larger space, say now,
"what a painful disgrace" that
I really wasn't fond of that place.

I heard a loudening boom
zooming across my room,
every time I saw her face.

I cannot now believe that
I never quite knew how to be
And how privileged I was to resume,

A life- hateful.

I'm amazed.

Currently Creating a Craze.

That has me so god damn dismayed that

the feelings I had were of hate.

I would cry every night in shame.

Putting every single blame on myself.   They were insane.

My mom making

my brothers godly saints

and my sister, the god damn maid. Yet

In The Night Only I Remained.

I know my room. My home. My space of comfort. The green carpet, the teal, Brown, and yellow walls were my home from age 15 on. I knew where to go. This huge room where I cried, cut myself, punched walls in rage, and felt all the pain that came from inside.

Mi Amor

He had to know what hurt me.

I was he
He was me

I couldn't show it, he could never know it.

And did I?

. . .

Trying to explain my relationship is trying to explain a toxic personality.

This Fucking Journey (Prior)

I had to have said "No" a hundred times.

Twirling
And
Twailing
My body to avoid contact.

3:00 in the morning
And he would not let me sleep!
The consequences of low-self-esteem.

I had broken up with my first love, Carlos Eduardo
One week Prior. Charlie Brown or
Carlos Moreno, where there was no fire.

I met him on Tinder,
Dropped me off at
Brew Monkey in the morning
And I felt raped.

I didn't say anything,
But I very much did . . .
I didn't talk to him again.

Until prom night

I was desperate, triggered, unknowing and unwilling to do my own healing.

So I called him.

He was absurdly misogynistic.

He got real butt hurt when I told him I was still in love with Carlos.

I got real butt hurt when he tried to fuck my ass without lube or my permission.

After High School graduation I moved into my sister's house and almost immediately began working at Denny's to prepare for college.

Meeting men from Tinder.

Turned on;   *wanting to say no-*

   Each time giving them what they wanted before we go.

After 3 months of money making waitress bullshit I moved into a one bedroom apartment with my brother.

 I slept on a made-up bed under the loft-bed of my brothers.

I had quit going to Westminster College, I
had some things to pay for. I was 19.

How did I make money?
Having sex with strangers.

The REASON

Charlie Brown took me to a party where I got an Underage Drinking Ticket that cost $800.

I gave $1,000 a month for 3 months that summer After High School toward attending Westminster College.

A month and a half into college and I couldn't pay for rent or food because I had given every last cent to that school.

Dave Ramsy taught my financial aid class in High School.
So I paid for everything   in cash
and dropped out the moment
                                                    I ran out.

I had been abusing my body anyway, so I might as well get paid for it.

Students start sex work to pay tuition at Westminster College
(Taken from the Westminster Forum) By McCall Mash on February 10, 2017

One October day, Lee dressed in high-waisted short shorts and a homemade striped crop top to meet Jay at a local coffee shop. They agreed to meet over coffee before Lee gave him the advertised $150 "fuck of his life."

Luckily, Jay offered Lee a drink after arriving at his place. She said alcohol makes people stupid, but she needed it, because she said fucking a guy she just met for money is also stupid.

After making sure she gave him exactly what he wanted, Lee said Jay took her out to dinner and then she went home—a typical day of work.

Lee, who asked The Forum not to use her last name for her protection, said she toyed with the idea of becoming a sex worker for months before she ever decided to do it. She would go on Tinder and ask her matches how much they would pay for sex—$50, $150, $200?

"I was trying to see my supply and demand," Lee said. "I was taking my macroeconomics class into my life," she added with a laugh.

lee said she felt like she wasn't in control of her sexual relationships and the lines of consent were often blurred, which is why sex work originally interested her.

"Money was the main reason, of course, but a lot of it was also my sex life at the time," Lee said. "I would sleep around a lot and I never felt like I was in control of whether or not we had sex because I wouldn't be able to say no, or let's go and so I would just have sex with all of these people and I felt like I was getting nothing in return at all."

However, after a string of events left her thousands of dollars in debt, Lee said she felt like the only option she had was to become a sex worker.

Before starting at Westminster College, the former first-year student was struggling to find a job and a secure place to live in Salt Lake City. Lee said she was stressed about paying tuition but wasn't too worried because her financial aid would cover most of the expenses. However, the Financial Aid Office informed her at the start of the Fall 2016 semester that her FAFSA didn't go through and that she owed the school more than double what she had already thought.

After discovering her FAFSA didn't go through, Lee said she wanted to escape her problems for a few days, which landed her uninsured and in the hospital.

"I took a lot of pills. I overdosed on a couple of pills. Not because I wanted to die; it was more like I just wanted to sleep for a couple of days and forget about my problems," Lee said. "So I purposely looked up enough to sleep for a while, and my brother freaked out and took me to the [emergency room]. And I don't remember it very well, but I was really pissed off that that happened because now I have $4,000 dollars of hospital bills for nothing."

After returning from the hospital, Lee said she wanted to go to her classes but struggled with attendance.

"When I came home, I couldn't go to school," Lee said. "I couldn't focus. I wanted to shoot myself in the face."

That's when Lee said she decided to become a sex worker, and she logged onto Tinder and began advertising to her matches.

Lee said, trailing off. . . **"Because you know, well fuck it. Literally fuck it."**

K A B

Taking you back to these times in truth.

Courage and forgiveness is with me,

Clarity is also our guide

As these memories are far suppressed and in need of releasing.

Understanding and forgiving is where I reside.

Let the past come forth in honesty, and pride-

from the perspective of only me this time.

Future and Disconnect
Strained Stress

As school was in session, my   to the people and knowledge.
energy soared

Future and disconnect strained *stress*.

So there it was?

The dehumanizing decision   a few times a day depending
to rape myself customers and   on the
how much they could pay?

Dehumanizing our true wants   for human connection and love
and desires
I separated myself from myself
for a   business.

It's "America". We do that all the time.

These memories are far   ready to be expressed now.
suppressed;

Protection of Forgiveness:

let the past come forth in honesty

as I reflect on this prominent and
immaculate piece of my life.

Reaching out

Reaching out came from deep within

Listen

like a pinny prick to confess a sin

Listen

I reached out to my ex-boyfriend

Trippin'

Although I didn't really see him

Listen

Clonazepam.

I was trippin'.

and

I swear

I saw you there.

My Intention Was To Become A Sex Worker

**Perhaps this was myself grabbing
this large problem and using it
for the greater evil of self-destruction...**

Death in the back of my mind, and knowing that would hurt my
loved ones,
my intention for taking 8 clonazepam that fall day was to fall
asleep.   Not to die.

To forget my trials,
To forget my decision to become a sex worker.
Reaching out.
Even as I was driven to the hospital-
reaching out.

I was in this position because of money and because of this
decision-

$4,000

fine

Upon awakening from the hospital **I had my first successful customer.**

Disconnected, I had to take control. Grab his neck. Kiss him all over like a long lost lover.

Afterward,

I was a   droggy   drone.

I wanted someone to cook and clean for me.
I wanted someone to clean my body.

The Faces

I don't know how to recall them all.
His, I definitely don't recall.

The gift fake orgasms cause

God-forbid I actually had one!

This Fucking Journey
When I Liked My Job

I went to this guy's house.
Drinking beer; and like most customers, did not have a particular fantasy to play out.

He was looking for a real human to fuck with no attachment.

However, he did not fuck me.
Lying on my stomach while he masterbaited to my ass for $150 was a 20 minute nap.

That one had me loving my job.

Only One More Compares

When I arrived I realized he had a broken leg and was wobbling around his house.

We tried to get situated in his bed and
I attempted to turn him on.

He was turned on enough to go inside for 6 seconds before saying,

"I'm too high" and,
"will you just walk my dog?"

He was $200 plus a bunch of "Thank you's" grateful for my service that evening.

This Fucking Journey
When I Didn't

I went on a call for a returner that made a fuss about paying before the sex because he didn't like "the paying thing".

I'll begin by describing our first encounter. This encounter being the "norm" in my experience, and then go on to tell a second encounter that was not as normal, and finally, give my profound life lesson from your local prostitute. (written for the Westminster Forum)

My customer replied to my message on Tinder and agreed on the $150 for "the fuck of his life". I dressed that October day of 2016 in high-waisted shorty shorts and a striped crop top that I made myself. We met at a local coffee shop that I walked to almost every day to meet customers.

I got in his very nice car and drove to his apartment. We walked in and luckily he offered me a drink. Alcohol makes people stupid; and it is my opinion that fucking a guy I just met for money, is really stupid.

A sober mind couldn't have had the vigorous sex I had with him, especially because he wanted to give me the money after we fucked. He highly enjoyed my dominance and equal submission that he did pay me, and advertised me to his friends.

Instead of taking me straight home, he took me out to eat, which was a common thing to happen.

Then I went home.

The second time we met was a little different. The first part was pretty much the same as the first time, up until after the sex was over. This is a night I am not proud of, and I'll blame it on intoxication.

After we were done having sex he wanted me to stay because I think he found joy in giving me more customers, like his roommate. When his roommate came in, he wanted me to stay naked for him, but I put on my thong and t-shirt. I couldn't have cared less if he thought I was worth the money or not based on my looks, because I know I am, in bed.

I am 5'6" and 150 pounds. I am floppy, not sturdy. I had a good habit of eating well and never working out at the time.
Except sex.

I flaunted around awkwardly because I wasn't drunk at all yet. My customer grabbed me in places showing his roommate, saying things like "oh is this sexy for you Jay?" and, "She's worth it", then turned to me, irritated, and in a demanding tone, telling me to "make him excited". I was nervous and awkward because I was uninterested in seducing someone to give up their money and have sex with me. So I just talked to Jay, "how's your day?", and normal conversation start-ups.

I will say that after this day my life could've been the American dream- if I was willing to give up my personality.

After drinking and getting touched everywhere by both of them, I was having fun. I was laughing and twerking and massaging them and snuggling up to the both of them. I was drunk then when my customer left to get another friend. I was all the more willing to cuddle with Jay. I tried to convince him to have sex with me but he refused to pay and that turned me on.

We had a very drunk conversation that I think really made him like me. It was about his daughter. I was actually pretty interested. I was also very drunk.

When my customer came back with a new friend, I realized where I was and the part I was playing: playhouse whore. I was drunk enough to go right back to it.

My customer was saying something about the guy who just came, and kept turning to me repeating, "don't worry about the money", so I thought, of course, this guy was going to pay for me. But these things aren't talked about a-matter-a-factly.

It wasn't until my mouth had already encircled this foreign penis, that I found out he wasn't paying. He, of course, tried to get me to continue. Disgusted and furious, I stormed out of the room and was embarrassed to be in front of Jay like that. The new stranger was mad and I was unable to make out real sentences. I was so mad, and drunk.

My customer drove the guy home due to his sketchy talk-about how my customer should pay for him and Jay and then they could all go at me at once.

I was then alone with Jay. I tried to get sympathy, but he didn't give any, saying, "You are an adult woman, you should've known better."

I certainly should have.

When my customer came back in he continued the same treatment of me: I became a nice piece of furniture he was showing Jay,

"It looks so nice, I love the way it feels right here, ooh and over here is very admirable, mmmm, [touch], mmmm [touch]" I finally I whispered timidly, "stop, I'm done," he either pretended or really couldn't hear me.

I said it again louder, with the same result. Then, my biggest achievement of the book: I demanded with all my might, "I'm done. stop touching me and give me my money!"

Jay then led me to his room where I found out what he wanted from me.

This part may not seem as disturbing to you, but this was the most to me.

He wanted me to spend the night and wait for him the next day while he was at work. He wanted me to not have sex with anyone but him. He wanted me to go to the spa all day- he talked about me getting my nails done and giving me an apartment- all ridiculous. His fucked up idea was to dress me up and have me there for him when he got home.

I will have sex with anyone for money before I get into a dependent relationship like that- to give up my soul, my personality, and everything I am just to live in ease. Hell no. We all work, we all give up hours of our lives to get the next paycheck so that we can survive. But to completely give up my day to day life, submissive, and depend on a man for my very own survival, is not at all what I want.

A lot of people take opportunities like this to survive; and they do survive, in the "all-mighty", consumer, capitalist luxury, we all fantasize about and love in the movies.

Not me, I will work and fight until my existence is my *own*.

This Fucking Journey

Mario and Luigi

They were two brothers, and for the sake of detachment,
I never actually remembered their names.

They were real live brothers.

One was short and one was "tall".

Mario was in charge.
"Take off your clothes. You, get on her."

It was always so uncomfortable and I just wanted to laugh at
them the whole time.

They called me a lot over the next few months.

$350

They were the fuckers I didn't like . . .

This Fucking Journey

Here Is One
That I did (sorta)

The man with red hair and a red beard touched my soul.

Trying to take his money and have sex with him, was not a pleasure,

He was conscious.

He wanted a real orgasm.

I'm disgusted by my lack of reciprocation.

Money hungry, my insensitive attitude ripped happiness on both ends.

Tearing us both into shamed, awkward realities.

This Fucking Journey

The Great Fall

A beautiful fall day.

He picked me up in a white car and drove me to his apartment.
He and I were both thinking, "What in the fuck am I doing?"

$40?

I was weaning off Venlafaxine at the time
and was given a very large weed cookie.

I said it would be a half an hour.

I also forgot about the tampon in my vagina until we started fucking.

Guess you get what you pay for.

I wanted to disappear . . .

And then I did

While being fucked
I was struck down
and displayed a vision.

Slowly losing control of my limbs
before everything went black.

I must have made sounds of terror because
the images were so clear in my head.

One by one they all came. Staring into my soul.

The faces of those who penetrated me penetrated me with their glare;

Their innocence, their humanity-
I didn't have much care.

After each face was shown they were shown again in a spiraling vortex
spinning me into

This Coma

My body became a myth.
My soul tormented my soul as I was helpless in attaching me
back to my body.
Swirling, tortured, and unable to move, the guy I was with
immediately stopped and put my clothes on for me. He got his
roommate to help him carry me down the stairs to the garage
with the white car.

He gave me his blanket, and left me where he found me.

Thank you for doing that whoever you are.
Your face and glasses in my brain.
You are a loving person, even though you took the $40 back,
it's all

the same.

Shave Shame

Stood up.

Again.

Shaved.

Shame.

I never

shaved

again.

.

Entitled Pain

I ask my friends, family, and all readers to take a moment

To forgive-
To place our hands on our pain

And maybe know we're all the same?

Thank you for supporting me in this game.

I thank you. I forgive me.

My choices, **my** self-harm, **my** pain.

Thanks again for supporting me. I respect and love you all so much for that. Only one more . . .

It Was Time to Tell My Sister and Stop

The very last story of sex is sad.

I knew I had created a living hell within myself
and I was ready to be done.

I invited my sister over to tell her.

> To stop.
> Me.

Unconscious that I had invited a customer over this day, I was walking outside my apartment doing my laundry when a stranger approached me. He asked, "Is that you?"

I looked at him funny. He said,

"You asked me to meet you here at this time to fuck."

Fuck.

"No." I said.
"I'm not doing that anymore."

"I came all the way out here, I have the money."
He shows it to me.

> **I now know shame creates spaces**
> **between boundaries**
> **caressing our faces with places**
> **we don't want to be in.**

We went to his truck.
I never fucked in a truck.
Fuck. The expression of words on a page will never truly emanate
the shame placed inside my brain from his penis into my body
when the words I said were "No" and I was still there.

                    The pain I felt formed more shame.

Submissive and lame

I am glad to be taking my time now to say,
yes, you weren't strong then.
But no, you will never be that weak again,
because you have grown.
Even though it's happened, even though

the situation has and will come up again
and again after this whoreable pain,
I am not ashamed.

I am not ashamed that I couldn't up and go,
I am not ashamed that I couldn't follow through with my "No".
Because I didn't know.

I didn't know that I could stand up and fight.
I didn't know that making them feel wrong was right.
I didn't know I had to practice might!

Because I wanted to die!

AND that is NOT the case anymore!!

I will not be IGNORED.

Not by myself.

Not by them.

No more.

I love myself and all these lessons I've learned

<u>I'm worth a stronger "No"</u>
And now

Know I am whole.

With help from my mother, financial aid reduced my hospital bill to $900, which I ignored for 6 months of prostitution, depression, self-growth, and falling in love with the very city, world, and body I despised.

A Dawn of a New Day, a New Light, a Dancing Star was Born

I was sitting in a coffee shop with a man who had paid me in weed for sex a month or so back.

He was a chill dude. I connected with him and we went geode hunting for Easter.

He owns a pond making business so
when 2 girls sat down across from us we
Had a healing cosmic meeting.

They invited us down the street to the Krishna Temple for a Permaculture meeting.

Over 30 adults in a circle conversate and ate.
                    Conversate and ate.
The Permaculture Community has forever grown seeds in
my heart that I need
                    More than anything.

Dance. Work. Dance. Sleep. Write music!

Scribble Scramble
I left turkey under my enamel.

Wiggle Waggle
The boys are baggled

Doodle daddle
They sip a swamble

And they all go tumbling toward Taylorsville.

Into Paiden's room

In this world where we have everything we have, I sat on my simple foam bed in a large decorated room across from Paiden's very big bed and I came to a realization.

What if all we want and all we need is just one connection, one trade away, and that everyone consumes much more than they pay, and if they just had something to do today, they wouldn't obsess over their story.

This was when my first inspiration for Education Guild came, and for me, it started with a no-monthly-payment lifestyle.

No phone payment. No rent. No car. Just life.

My Plan Was This:
- Give phone away
- Sell car-$
- Passport/visa?
- Give clothes and possessions away
- Durable waterproof pants
- Awesome backpack
- Awesome coat
- New glasses

And to achieve this: a Bike Trailer!

Why did I have this dream?
What brought to pass this unconventional fantasy of living with no money?

College did. Westminster did. Life did. Who are humans who live paycheck to paycheck supposed to do to get out of this hole?

College?

That almost put me $40,000 a year into the hole
I sold my soul to sex just to pay for.
Not to mention food and rent and holy fuck did I want to kill myself. The entire system is wack and what are we, were we and will we do about it?

With so many false beliefs and illusions surrounding the culture of needy attachment: capitalism; there has to be another way.

Detachment,

Getting out of the box- toward one another- and I believe it is to be rid of the world's curse creating illusions of separateness and lack of opportunity so certain people can get much more from others.

I am here to give and take.
Not to be a fucking number of monetary value.

I say this in anger, anger stemming from shame in the sadness I carry because I am about to spend all of my paycheck on a car I "Have" to have to have a paycheck.

See the contradictions? The loops? The holes we are all in because of this tool, this fantastic way to consume much more than we can pay?

The enabling. The enabling of spending. The conditioning of spending. The fact that every human on this Earth has to find a way to make enough any way they can, no matter what it takes-advantage.   Letting go of dreams.

How on Earth can we go on like this?

We are killing our mother!   We are taking advantage of her!

Then,

Aspiring this no-monthly-payment lifestyle,

I moved into my car with a boy named Jon boy.

As winter approached

We went to the source
Of Jon boy's childhood.

R.I.P Isaac

Jon boy and I had love for each other and had such a fun experience turning my little Kia Forte into a real home with insulation, curtains and a semi-comfy bed (especially comfy when it was just one person sleeping in it). It was a beautiful experience. I learned a lot about listening to myself, whom I tended to ignore.

Before Jon boy and I moved into the car, I remember drinking a lot of coffee at Kathy's house, where I worked with her son, and, as I traveled home, was very high from it.

I was freaking out because I had just made the decision to move into a car with Jon boy.

I walked into the house where I was sharing a room with my wonderful friend Paiden.

Our roommate Isaac was cooking.
I started chatting with him.

I found myself in a craze as I had to stop myself from saying what felt like was shouting at me, "YOU WANT TO TRAVEL WITH ISAAC, NOT JON BOY!"

However loud the voice kept screaming at me was, I didn't listen, and around April of 2018, Issac went missing in the Colorado mountains, never to be heard from again.

I touched his arm
and we
started living
in a car together?

I Was Never Actually His GIrlfriend

I knew instantly doing Acid with his friends all night long was a bad decision.

Acid is such a connecting drug.

I had a fantastically hard time. I felt blocked from connecting with all of his friends because I felt like I was "Jon boy's girlfriend" to them. I never felt real awkward before in my life.

He knew that I felt our relationship was in time and would not be forever. This is what he did not listen to. This is where I found life so difficult with Jon boy; because I didn't want myself split in half.

I wanted friends- I wanted his guy friends to be my friends, I wanted to feel like a whole person, my own person, not someone's girlfriend, especially his. Not that he isn't a dope dude, just not for me.

Visiting Utah for Christmas

I totally totalled our house-car.

Then we totally caught a ride to Jon's Grandparents house from my brother on the sixth of January 2018.

I was to cook.

Jon boy was to fix things.

And if he didn't, his grandma slapped him!

So we moved into our own apartment.

$1200 a month for a room in a condo is very cheap for Mountain View CA.

We had parties daily and I started Education Guild there with all my amazing friends.

Education Guild is a free space to communicate and learn more with each other.

But

It didn't last long . . .

Because

I needed

Space.

So Jon Boy Left That Place

And I had a crush on someone. So
After living and working together for 5 months, Jon boy was
picked up by a friend and taken back to Utah.

The attachment monster inside of me told Jon boy,
"I want to kill you," and then
the surrender to the individual that I am became clear once again.

In the span of 2 weeks, while he was preparing to leave,
I created the dream
I had been fantasizing about and planning for every day before
meeting Jon boy.

And with the help of his grandpa Rudy, Anup, and Spade, I made
a 5'3'4' bike trailer.
I planned to hook onto the back of the black beautiful bicycle I
bought for $900 and travel the world.

I walked my 35 pound homemade trailer 8 blocks to my friend
Syd's front driveway.

It had everything I owned in it.

It felt so good to get away from that $1,200 one bedroom off
Bush St.

CLC

The palm trees lining the streets of the quiet masterminds of
money- activists for activity and active minds-
I once got free orange juice and social time
on my bicycle ride to the Creative Learning Center where I worked.

I biked to work then biked to work then biked home.

And when I didn't have the money, I would busk on Castro St.

I would also bike the opposite direction on the weekends going
into the Moffett Field Base.

Where I would walk with a peer.

He's non-verbal and full of energy.

And we were very connected.

He once did Yoga with me on his own!

Because I was doing my own Yoga,
super chill, on the grass, in my zone,

he started to do his

own Yoga!

When I had to move my trailer to a space in between this Starbucks and 7-eleven,
his mom was uncomfortable with my situation.

I was having a blast-   drum-circle/open-circle
                                              Every Night.

Love you, Danny!!!!!

But she still convinced me to move it into her garage.

It was so stuffy.
And so not fun.

I literally needed no money!

Which was great.

SO MUCH GRATITUDE!!!!!

The Last Time I Did Acid. /
My First Bike-Packing Trip.

"If I was to see my mother . . . I would hold her, get to know her, tell her that I love her."

"To organize my thoughts of literature literally litters a little bit."

"I think Poison Ivy is the Placebo effect."

"Goal: Become BFFs with anybody. Lol. Now I feel like BFF's with Everybody!"

Then I left,
biked down the West Coast.

The End.

When Jesus Took Me To Roosevelt

When Jesus Took Me to Roosevelt

Who am I in the picture story of Jesus healing the people?
I am Jesus, You are Jesus- we are the healers,
the humanity and humility to be healed by each other.

What a powerful blessing to be human!

The truth is I have no Story.
I am alive here every moment.

and I do what feels right.

The truth is I am you. I am everything.

I am everyone and every experience ever to experience.

I've seen the things I've seen;
You've seen the things you've seen.

and with two   different   sides
Since
If no one else saw it

Is it reality?
Truth?

I AM today.

                    This is how I'll stay.

A Transition Statement:

From Mountain View, CA
To Roosevelt, UT

I knew right away why their son was unhappy.

The invisible and powerful force of anger, frustration, and annoyance is
too much for most people to bear.

His autism heightened senses.

He was very much aware.

There was no way I was going to go to college and stay emotionally suppressed.

So I left.

Imaginary strings attached me to the sands of Mitchell Murray's 2 ½ acre land.

The book I was reading on how to make a self-sustaining ¼ acre and

The dreams I envisioned while sitting on the couch of the Tosas' family's house while watching their lives play out.

Mitchall Murray's Property

My Brother, his girlfriend, and I arrived at Mitchell Murray's property after dark.
Evan's girlfriend had to leave very early so I asked if I could stay and be picked up in 4 days.

My phone, left dead in the car.

DAY 1:

I hear the animals. Eat one bite of pizza every few hours. Some peanut butter here and there. Indica to nap through the hours- to avoid heat.
I dreamt of a tall woman with long, black hair who walked straight onto the property yelling, "Friend! I'm here to make friends!". She was so cute. We were friends.
As my mind clears from the weed of the day, the sun is beginning to set. No need. Breath. For this world is mine.

In conclusion with the sun setting:

How great it is to be.

Day 2:

1 jar of peanut butter. 1 slice of pizza. Sardines. Honey.

Yummy.

Today the sun touches the earth so gently.
He feels every beam with the sand.
Rocks and Sagebrush caressing the light,
the sand is tickled by the little red ones and awoken by
the   ever-so-sleepy-sun   -
still right behind the clouds.

The misty light finally emerging from sleeping in.

1. Rock collecting 2. Trash compiling 3. Shower

$\frac{2}{3}$ done.

What can I say but today I breathed and ate sardines; worked with
my back and played a tune;
        thought maybe I'd try to masturbate soon.

....

....

....

....

....

....

....

....

....

....

....

....

....

....

....

Day 3

Halfway through. Tuesday. Peanut Butter Tuesday.

Challenge: Flies.

When I invite them, they come, and when I tell them "No" they go for my face.

So *I decided it tickles,*

Now flies make me laugh.

I found a can of chili in the garbage I went through . . .

I trust myself and love myself!

Yay! Hunger no more!

Hunger Rumbles: *I am doing this for myself and for the land.*

Day 4!

I still have quite a lot of energy. I need to remember food is good.

Just once, 3 times a day.

   My body.

It feels good to listen silentlee at what my body is telling me.

This life is not a one way street, it can be taken in every
                                        which
                                                direction.

   A hummingbird flew right under the gazebo. Right next to me. Blue, green, and shiny.

   I knew Evan would be there.
   I went to go meet him
   at the time it was.
   Not to be disappointed-
   I walked in the *opposite* direction.

      When I heard the honk I ran back.

Seeing Jesus

I walked down the street from the Krishna Temple to the Greenhouse Effect Open Mic Night.

I was jamming outside when Haven and this white man, Riley Workman- with a long blonde Afro, silky robe, universe pants, and a universe tank top walked up to me.

We stared into each other's eyes.
Without question, without word;

Stared, trusted, loved, then hugged at our first meeting.

What an experience meeting love and light themself before their comical and passionate speech about how they were Jesus Christ!

Only difference is their white.

Riley, Haven, and I returned to Dalton's house after our performances- both being improv- and with one kiss on the lips from each of them, we rested well.

When we awoke, Riley and I walked
around Salt Lake City.

We sang.
I danced.

We had a very nice day.

He made a Youtube video next to the Mormon Temple and I reassured the concerned lady Missionary that he was with Me.

Well played...

We discovered his desires & mine aligned at that specific time because he had space for my bike and he wanted to finish up a video at his cabin in Tabiona just a few towns east of Mitchell Murray's Property.

Riley Entered Ali and Chad's home, where I was honored to stay while living on my bicycle, with an,

"It is I! Riley!"

I love in Riley. We pulled the lovers card that night at Daltons.

On our way to Roosevelt we stopped at a coffee shop in Heber where He asked, "What do you want from me?" and I asked, wanting only love and support,
"Will you hold my hand?" and we held hands while listening to the song on the coffee shop radio,

And stared.

"What's going on in your beautiful mind, I'm on your magical mystery ride and I'm so dizzy, don't know what hit me but I'll be alright. Cards on the table were both showing hearts . . ."

And stared.

We went to the water.
We went to the sand.
Where he then left me on Mitchell Murray's land.

I howled to the moon,
And saluted the sun.

And you are me and we are one.

The night was luminous, with an over-sensing sense of hereness.

Healing

It comes without word,

                                    listen
They are feelings- but really,

                        listen
They do speak.

Every bit of the body speaks.
                                    listen

Vibrating each chakra- seeing colors and shapes;

The Flower.

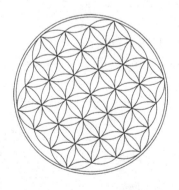

I know myself much better now.

Alone

When alone with myself I'm never alone.
When I let myself go,

I know.

I hear, I see, and communicate with me.

ME: source.

I called it cerebral, my brain in your brain.

The one that when I was alone never

                              once

                    called

                                        me

        insane.

Just Be with Lee,

A re-treat.

Just Be. LEE Bee. Beeing busy & being.
Being Lee B is to Be.

Maomi painted the cutest bee I'd ever seen.

With $500 and nothing to take care of but myself, I wanted this bee as a tattoo.

I thought about my living situation.

A 5 gallon tank of water on top of a cup dispenser used as a sink.

Recycled recycling bin from Jordan Valley School, used as a water trapper & for our compost.

A fire pit, Gazebo, and A tent full of cute mice and scorpions.

Lizard friends abundantly bouncing on their hands.

Bathing, running, eating, and being.

The Woods, The Cabin, The Hill Up Top. The People, The Spirit of Those On Top.

There were 2 events that I had to learn from in order for this particular transition from city to country to happen smoothly:

1- Ali & Chad's knowledge of the trigger: emotions being triggered by the outside world.

2- Paiden's parents' AA retreat, "Believe"- where I was majorly triggered.

1-

While staying at Ali and Chad's home for a week when living on my bicycle in SLC

We were all triggered every day.

As we all are.

And being aware of when and why we were being triggered was our daily practice.

2-

With an undying love for my old roommate Paiden,

I went to the AA retreat she invited me to in order to let go of my
Addictions to bad food and the fear of being myself.

On our way to the retreat, the door of the coffee shop cut my
ankle deep enough to bleed all over the sidewalk.

That was the moment I knew the retreat wasn't going to go well.

A brilliant scenery. A conundrum. I don't think I was ever rude.

The snacks, the donuts, the carnivorous food.

It was when we were on the 6th of the 12 steps that I began to
know why fear, sadness, and confusion filled everyone's eyes.

We started circling a list of bad qualities that we were.

I immediately felt like all those bad qualities were all lies, that
that was not me, and I was, in fact, a really good, honest, sincere
feeling person.

 Dwell on my negative sides and eat sugar filled snacks?

"Step down, let Jesus be the leader of your life"-
 the themed phrase.

Pretend to be too far gone, and step down?
I was absolutely amazed.

Doing my best to be myself, saying as I felt,
knowing I'm okay, and I have things to say.

Like
I don't believe Jesus can possibly lead the way.

His idea- a spirit, a light, maybe.

But stepping down, at that time, did not feel okay.

My intention was to spend time with Paiden, not to give my life to Jesus.

And denying being a stoner at all, is actually none of anyone's business.

                                                              Good call.

Cause when the devils of control and power gave their sacred prayer:

"Do you accept Christ as the leader of your life?"
They asked Paiden
while holding her head back.

I heard the Silent Power of her personal prayer Screaming,
"I BELIEVE IN SPIRIT," as she felt, and instead expressing,
"Yes," as she cried.

I felt my own spirit pounce.
How could you? I silentlee asked these oppressors of opinions.

Then verbally,
"I am Jesus Christ. He is Me. And he is with me when I say,
I AM THE POWER!"

With my arms outstretched like a falcon, this I know. This I was.
This I am.

Like a fiery phoenix against this crazy clan.

I spent my time at this retreat expressing my love and gratitude for every person I could, being triggered, and crying.

We are divine and unknown, to be questioned and grown.

Not to be reaped of our life with plants that "Jesus" sown.

Growing up, all our thanks be to god, and
I didn't get enough attention.

So as words of nonsense go,
Upon the land I wish to sow,
As I track the undertow of

Greatness above and
Respect below.

A mystical enchantment of flourishing fields

Hunting each other's madness reveals

The strength of humans

above and below.

Bluebell

The first time I went to town, I went right, to Bluebell's beautiful restaurant/gas station- the only store in town.
The hill was killer, the view was stellar.

On my way back I went to Stevin's house to shower, the only other person Mitchell Murray and I knew. He was our neighbor right up Bluebell Road.

I did feel the sexualization of my perceived gender when going to Stevin's house.

I seemed to set pretty clear boundaries.
His son was a meth-head- susceptible to spiritual shit.
Later, he helped me fix my bike.

x

Now I See What I Felt

The second time I went to any town, I made a left turn to Roosevelt, ten miles away, looking to do laundry. My very first stop was at Cedar Bear where Amber led me to the cure for my sinuses.

While doing my laundry I checked out the tattoo shop where I met Justin and Sue. Then down to Mama Lia's, I couldn't believe the free food!

Then when charging my phone at Marions, they gave me a burger I highly recommend.

They seemed Ute represented, but something was off.

The Uintah Basin. Once home, now as their reservation, the white man wanted the land for oil.
Pressed.   And more.
                              My bike started to sound weird . . .
Back to the Frontier Grill.

With this weird sound, a want for adventure, and the only bike shop 20 miles away in Vernal; I had come to town that day wondering if the tables would turn or if I would ride away- Vernal to Colorado then beyond
on that September day.

Creator created my stay

I had biked from the sands of the cove to eat a salad.

I was sitting and eating food when a typical old cowboy proclaimed,
"Hey, It's the Biker Girl!"

We heard each other through our eyes.

When he left, I ate and sat.
Not knowing his plan.

He then sent in
the first lazy-eyed human
of Roosevelt
to meet me.

                      The stars aligned.
We were instantly friends.

This beautiful soul. "Erin Ilene" she said,
"Do you need a bed?"

                      I nodded my head.
She had a spare room for me.

I wanted a tattoo.

She needed a new phone.

So I started a yoga class.

It was abundantly clear to me we had the same goals of healing and love.

Her scars run far-
deep in her past.

Reopened.

I look back now through the eyes of compassion.

I do take this story with passion.
Because it's so uncomfortable.

"Why do I bring it up?"
I hear myself say.

Because it's Processed Suffering,
not to evade.

Roosevelt City

When Mitchell and I first went to the property he was already there staying at a hotel, my phone was dead.

I had written down instructions to get to the hotel, a three hour chance, but after Biking 600 miles, it was another beautiful illusion of what we humans can do.

190 miles in a car was a refreshing eye opener of life, privilege, knowledge, space, and time.

I got there no problem.

The only time fear was in my presence was when I missed the exit to Heber.

I knew I did, so I checked with the lady at the gas station. She told me,

"You'd better be careful out here by yourself."

The fuck?

People live out here.

No one told me that riding a bike through Los Angeles, Santa Cruz, or San Diego.

Y'all Harvest Rapist out here?

Cause there were men all around when that lady said that.

Speaking of Men

When I got to the hotel after a blind 3 hours in the starry night, I found myself in Mitchell Murray's hotel bed.

He went straight for my vagina.

So I took it to my face

and jacked him off.

Thank god.

Being Naked

I was naked with Mitchell Murray

I was naked doing work.

I was naked when Erin came to the property,

she asked about my sex life with a shmirk

"You'd use my masturbater later," she said,
"and I'd hear you,
bang down the door,
then you can't say 'no'."

I don't know if Erin Ilene could possibly know . . .

How unsafe that made me feel
Living in her home.

Y'all just wanted to feel pleasure,

But no thanks!

Not at my expense!

On the property I felt the sand delivering messages of history.

So much pain. So much inflicting pain. It was no mystery.

A divide.

I channeled and knew what had happened there before it was affirmed. Inherited into me, this country, and this town: Racism.

Erin Illene said, "Don't go on the reservation or you'll get raped."

Saying nothing was my reply . . .

And she wasn't the only one in Roosevelt assuming the worst of Natives. . .

Flipping forward to Maui March 2020 where some white people told me,
"don't go to Haleakala, or they'll eat you" … … … literally.

Pappy's

My Favorite Restaurant to go to was Pappy's.
It was spacious, had a stage, and absolutely amazing workers.

Out of the 7,000 people in this town, three were the most
frequent customers:
Tom, Wayne, and Me.

Here is my Monologue about it:

Ello, my name is Lee.
I wanted to express myself today. And it may be in an angry
sort of way,
Because I have something extremely important to say.

I am wondering if I am being seen,
Because these two particular old men at Pappys got really mean
and I believe it all started with them not seeing ME.

Do you see me as I see you?

Human,

Dining at the restaurant on Lagoon.
Misusing those serving YOU.
I was taught to say "please" and "thank you". Never to boss, and
demand what to do.

Did you hear me singing Wayne?

I was in the back of the room.
It was quite a lovely tune.

Or were you really that confused
why I'm not out with my "oil rig" dude?
"I don't want cancer" was my defense, however rude, but I only
said that because I don't want to be abused.

Not not seen, not not heard, not misused, because
I thought you may say something like, "hey that was a good
song; tell me how you get along?" but I guess you hearing or
seeing anything from me was where I went wrong.

And how about you, old man Tom, did you see me?
Or were you blinded by my body?

I thought that after I sang you that personal song, we may actually
get along. After I played the guitar and sang, you told me about
your past wife, and I really felt your pain. And as soon as I turned
my back, please tell me I was wrong, cause I swear I heard your
thoughts as clear as day and it wasn't because of my missing bra, it
was because the very next time I saw you when I tried to say, "hey",
you said you'd "only recognize me with my clothes off" and that
really put me to shame. You were there too, weren't you, Wayne?

You guys.

I just want you to know that I see you.

I hear you.

I'm conscious of everything you say, everything you do, and I'm not here to play along and allow those thoughts and obsessions to go on, I was there to sing a song!
To express myself, to live, come on! I know you saw me Tom.

I saw you as a friend.

Which is why I am doing this; because I treat my friends with honesty, and honestly? That behavior has to end.

Because I heard you when you told MY FRIEND, YOUR waitress that she'd "better sit on his [Wayne's] face" and I know you heard me when I told you that was "sexual harassment" and I definitely heard you when you told me to "speak up like a white man".

My feminine side may have answered you then.   (silence)

But I have two sides, Tom.
And without balance my life will go all wrong.

So this time. Here is my manly reaction. Because this man named Lee will take action. He will speak like the "white man" that I am because I can.

Because ALL humans have the right to express!

So get ready Tom, for this gender-fluid HUMAN
to speak up.
For their voice will shake your very soul.
Their voice will devour your pride.

You will hear ME.
You will see ME.

My words will spark the thought in your mind that

YOU ARE NOT THE ONLY ONE IN THE ROOM and
YOU ARE NOT ENTITLED TO THE WOMEN AROUND YOU!

This time Tom, I will sing a tune so full of you that your heart will ache to sing it too
and frantically chase itself around the room screaming, "you can't let this girl through! What are you doing, what are you?"

Who are you?

And I'm serious, Roosevelt, when I say,
that is NOT "waitress culture"
that is RAPE culture.

And it doesn't have to be this way because I am here today and I will not be the laughing or silent enabler of their disgusting behavior.

I am their equal in this life and will let them know the truth that I said no.

No.

I will not be your little mind fantasy thing!

I have stories to tell, I have songs to sing!

I will not be silenced by your enabled upbringing.

I AM HERE

I WILL SING.
I WILL SPEAK.

And it's up to you whether or not I am seen.

Thank you.

Yoga, Meditation, and Creation w/ Lee

My first encounter with Erin Ilene was
powerful, and psychic.

She was the stranger that walked into the bathroom and
was peeing while I was washing up.

Since she's a trucker-

She knows what it means to take a shower in the bathroom.

Erin Ilene and I decided to meet back at the Frontier Grill at 5:00
pm that night.

When she left to get her phone,
I was curious to see what the town had for me.
I went to the tattoo shop where I met Sue and talked about my Bee.

Leaving the tattoo shop I started Biking down the street.

I saw David outside his Jiu Jitsu studio.
He was moving from one place to another and we agreed that I
could teach yoga there for free.

We decided that 8 pm every night after Jiu Jitsu would be
Meditation W/ Lee.

He asked about my credibility,

I simply stated that I was dedicated to the healing of my Body
and felt called to help others hear theirs.

Josiniah

I had been spreading the word about my yoga class when some dwarpy emoji man came out of the smoke shop as I was walking by.
He asked me if I had a lighter. I said no, and invited him to yoga.

We slapped and snapped.

My first yoga class was a private healing session with Josiniah, the emoji man.

On the floor I had him lay
and saw his cringed up face
as I told him he was safe.

When we made eye-contact
I could see the monster he thought he was-
Destroying his space, memories, with the lack of loving embrace.

I immediately knew why I was sent to this place.

On the second day of yoga Josiniah brought his friend, Jaiden.

The third was with Jaiden, Josiniah, Mary, Joe, Starlight, and Sunbeam.

Biking home that night was exhilarating.

                                                        Powerful.

My eyes were open to all the vibrations of the universe.

                        There was a trigger, however unnecessary
                                and shifting, meant to Be.

I said, "and the next time you guys come if you could Bring a donation that would be great!"

Don't tell defiant teenagers to pay for their presence.

So on the fourth day of Yoga, Meditation, Healing, and Creation with Lee, I was surprised to see that
it was just Josiniah and me . . .

Preparing for the lesson earlier, I had seen someone post about human touch on social media.

Having not had much human touch at the time,
I had planned for us to massage each other's hands.

But he was the only one there,
he said he cared, and
Called me cute.

I felt his skin brush against my skin
I stared in his eyes, saw the love within
Only once did his eyes scream "SIN"

:The first poem made in Josiniah's home of Roosevelt UT.
The last poem I wrote about Josiniah in Roosevelt UT:

SIN

Why am I so scared of Sexual INteraction ?
What's made me not want to share this action
with any real human except him and porn?
Should I date a lot of guys to see who I can scorn?
See what sights are within,
See new heights from the sin?
Or is it the sin to obsess over something so detest I'd rather
lose than win?
Have I got a candidate and a prize?
Or maybe it's his size?
I could talk to many guys
But I feel like they'd all be lies
Because with you I'd truly win.
So is that a sin?

Sex

Is

Not

To be fucked with.

Lee's Timeline
of Small Town
Homelessness:

-Erin Ilene- fleeing.
>   (she had to go trucking)
-Josiniah's house- draining.
>   (He had such creepy demons)
-Second Time Around- paying
>   (Rob let me stay in their cute loft apartment)
-Nics house- truly living.
>   (the second lazy-eyed human I just adore, miss you)

Eventually I had to get a "real" job.

GREATEST ACCOMPLISHMENTS: Bicycled 600 miles down the coast of California alone. Spent weeks alone; living and breathing the sun on my friend's property near Roosevelt as a personal retreat before either going on another bike tour or starting a yoga class in town; I chose to stay in Roosevelt. I am 21 years old, I have 15 nieces and nephews, and have worked with children and those with special needs for 6+ years. I am a happy, aware human and I value each of my past jobs and relationships above all, leaving only because of a new living situation as I discover the true meaning of working and living for myself.

Con Amore

When I applied and took a tour of the school,

I ended up seeing my teacher from my Jr. High School when I peer tutored for special needs as a teen.

The Principal walked me into her classroom and that being my very first credential, I started my job doing substitute PE.

I did courses and yoga for the classes that came in, and when I started as an aide I would always do yoga and meditate in the gym after school.

So I opened up the class for the teachers,

t it didn't really last with my anxiety, I made a flier to earn some money that I never passed out:

Hello! My name is Lee.
My pronouns are he/she.
I love to sing, write, dance,
And be.
Experiencing life in my own unique way.
I am 21 and I've been a Paraprofessional,
Paraeducator, and now, an Aide.
And I've never quite known where to
Stop, and stay.
Until now,
Where I truly believe I've
been called today.

So if you feel called, this is cheap to pay,
Feel free to leave early,
and show up late.

Con Amore

Nic was gay and took me to church.

I was so honored to live in his home, with his two cats, two dogs, one ferret, six chickens, lots of plants and produce, and the coy fish in my room.

He blessed me with my most cherished memories- with him, and Arts Kids. I hold nothing dearer to my heart.

Reserved only because of reservations- the Ute Native tribe stays strong- liberation banging at the door of all of mamma- and so much more . . .

The Episcaple Church in Whiterocks, I just adore, held a weekly after school program called Arts Kids where up to 50 Ute kids would meet in Whiterocks to set intentions, make art, and eat dinner.

My life in Roosevelt was practically perfect.

Setting intentions, and meeting them.

Expressing our feelings. . .

Reserved only as an effect of reservations

I had two amazing jobs.

Did yoga three times a week at least.

Taught classes too!

It sparked so much joy in my life, seeing joy in theirs.

Learned where I need to grow- by listening.

Thank you Sue for your beautiful love.

Thank you Forest for your healing horses and precious land.

Thank you Nic for making me a part of your family.

Thank you Micheal for your kind support.

Thank you Gumby Yoga for trusting me to teach "Just Be With Lee", where I ate an orange sitting, watching the sun, instead of teaching; awkwardly leaving them to do their own thing.

Thank you to the Indigenous tribes in Utah for your connection to this piece of mother earth.

I'm so sorry my blood participated in reserving you, holding you back from being and being you.

Your liberation isn't mis-taken.

Flash forward 4 years when I came back to visit. . .

The billboards

The building

All changed

In the way

I manifested.

The billboards went from one saying:
"the ONLY woman OBGYN doctor" with a picture of her, and
then the very next one:
"the BEST OBGYN doctors" displaying 4 white males . . . To:

"Native American POWER" where before the tribe called
themselves "Ute Indians"

I'm very proud of you.
Thank you.

Feb 24, 2019

Today I dreamt about an overnight care facility for special needs. I woke up & got up to see the time- first 24 hours without my phone- woke up Nic- then went back to sleep.
Woke up to Nic, Fishy's, and coffee.
Smoked a bowl, ate Raisin Bran and went to church.

Who am I in the picture story of Jesus healing the people? I am Jesus, You are Jesus- we are the healers and the humility to be healed by each other.
What a powerful blessing to be a human.

Bloody Vagina Monologue
written by Nic Rich

The Jazz music is poping
And Lee's vagina is slurping, and this moment is perfect,
blub blub . . . slap slappity slap!

Free is Lee and her vagina is free to be seen.

The jazz music is poping
and bees vagener is
slurping and this mament
is purfect Blab Blab...
slap slapty slap! pree
is bee and her vagener
is pree to Be seen.
Blbadly vaginer monolog.

Printed in the United States
by Baker & Taylor Publisher Services